NAVIGATING THE PITFALLS OF LIFE

Betrayed by Marriage

Valerie Ovington

Copyright © 2023 (Valerie Ovington)
All rights reserved worldwide.

No part of the book may be copied or changed in any format, sold, or used in a way other than what is outlined in this book, under any circumstances, without the prior written permission of the publisher.

Publisher: Inspiring Publishers,
P.O. Box 159, Calwell, ACT Australia 2905
Email: publishaspg@gmail.com
http://www.inspiringpublishers.com

 A catalogue record for this book is available from the National Library of Australia

National Library of Australia The Prepublication Data Service

Author: Valerie Ovington
Title: Navigating the Pitfalls of Life: Betrayed by Marriage
Genre: Nonfiction / Memoir

Paperback ISBN: 978-1-923087-65-1

CHAPTER 1

My parents married 6 February 1929. First son born 5 November 1929, second son January 1932. First daughter born March 1933 and second daughter Born February 1935. Mum and Dad thought their family complete. Two sons and two daughters. But not to be. Another son born February 1939 and four daughters February 1941, July 1943, myself July 1946 and finally my sister July 1948.

Having three children born the middle of winter took it's toll on my mother's health and she was hospitalised for quite some time after my youngest sister's birth. My two older sisters took the responsibility of our everyday needs. Which would have been a burden for these young fifteen and thirteen year old teenagers.

My eldest brother helped my father keep the farm producing as there would have been mortgage payments to be met. My other brother at the age of sixteen went to live and work on a neighbouring farm. They had just the one child a son about the same age. My brother would have enjoyed the peace and quiet of a small family away from the hustle and bustle of our large one.

My eldest brother did not have the interest of being a farmer. He wanted to be an engineer. His hobbies were pulling machinery apart and putting them back together to understand the mechanics of their function. But he sacrificed that ambition to help our father on the farm without little payment. Our father did appreciate his loyalty to us all.

I have a vague memory of my older siblings being excited when a strange woman turned up in our house. Turned out to be my mother coming home after a long convalescence. This probably caused the separation anxiety I developed, and I became very attached to my mother during my childhood. But on the plus side I was a loyal companion when I felt necessary to be and could step aside when that person no longer needed me.

My eldest sister married at the age of eighteen years. She like her older brother probably needed to escape the large family turmoil. The marriage was a disaster. Her husband was in his thirties and seen himself as a playboy. They had been married for just six months when he started bringing home his lovers. My sister would have had to take a step back from what she expected the roll of a wife was. Nobody prepares us for a life with a Narcissist. She had her first child eleven months after her marriage. She did move back with our family for a while. But had to eventually return to her lecherous husband. That was the expectations in those days. Empathy to another human's rights was not ever considered at this period of our history.

She did eventually escape this disaster of a marriage after the birth of another daughter and two sons and several attempts on her own life. Our parents bought her a lovely new house. I guess they owed her that after the help she gave the family in their time of need.

I know I was grateful and stepped in at the end of my parents' life to change my father's will to include her in our inheritance as equal share. Some of my siblings thought my interference unfair as she had been given a house. But we were all given opportunities which she did not get.

CHAPTER 2

My school day started early as we travelled six kilometres to school in a horse drawn sulky. During the winter months we would be rugged up with old blankets and a brick which we heated in the oven. We had a wood burning stove which was great in the winter but overheated the kitchen in summer when it had to be kept fired up as it was the only source of cooking and heating water. During the year 1956 the wettest year on record for this area. The constant days of sitting in class in wet clothes led to my body succumbing to a bout of Pneumonia and I ended up spending some time in Hospital. Farmers were having a hard time of getting their harvest completed so my father was away a lot helping. Because of the wet impassable dirt roads my illness became serious but eventually I got help. Fortunately for me Penicillin was available. At this time Penicillin was injected into the body, Oral medication wasn't available.

My first year of school we met with an accident. My siblings would pick up their friends on the way to school. Our horse was the Waler breed, patient and calm. But on this morning a group of children waited until we drove into the school gate and jumped out and startled the horse. He bolted breaking the strap that connected him to the sulky. I landed first with a few bodies landing on top of me. Not sure but that experience may have set of my dislike to enclosed space.

There also was a practice by the older boys of untying the horse during our lunch break with the idea of getting out of class in the afternoon to go and fetch it. One day this practice led to an unfortunate accident. The horse got tangled in a fence and sustained a very bad cut to one leg. Fortunately, my father inherited from his parents the excellent knowledge of healing and the horse made a complete recovery.

In the meantime, we drove a young Waler horse which our dad tried to train as a trotter, but he broke the trot and kept being disqualified. The horse had a competitive nature, and we had some very fast and bumpy trips to and from school. We did get back our old faithfully eventually.

I loved school and learning all about the world outside my small, introverted life on an isolated country farm. I revelled in the competition of getting high results in exams. I inherited this from my hardworking parents. They married just before the Great Depression and WW2. My father worked as a share farmer during the day and night shift in a Cannery to help feed the fighting forces overseas. My mum kept the homelife in order. She came from a farming background and new the ways of preserving food and making jams. Great cook and was an asset to my father with her knowledge of finance. The opportunity to purchase a run-down farm after the war and turning it into a high producing enterprise with help from my siblings. This was the example set for me to live up to.

At the age of 15 years my parents took me to visit my father's sister. She and her husband had offered to adopt me and give me the opportunity to further my education. Because my other siblings had never been given these choices, I was to be given away to another family member, so it didn't appear unfair to them. I was lucky to be given a chance but turned it down. I could not leave my family.

I furthered my education by completing a business practice certificate at the local Technical College. Subjects being typing, shorthand, book-keeping etc.

I worked at the local cannery during the summer school break with my two older sisters who assisted me in navigating to working life. The money saved went towards the cost of fees and books for my course. I went on to work as a junior with the Water Marketing Council. Then onto The Rice Marketing Board as a receptionist.

I moved to a larger city with more opportunities at the age of twenty years. Women's wages were low at this time and paying rent and buying food did not leave much over for any thing else, but it taught me lessons for my future survival. I was lonely at first, the locals were a clicky bunch as is most populations that grow together from school and maintain contact with each other.

I met a young man that was in a similar situation to me as he had moved from his family town to study in Wagga. He was in an occupation that would take him around the world, and we would be constantly moving. I confided in some of my siblings and the response was unanimous. That lifestyle would not be suitable for me. I was confused as I thought that something that felt so good was not to be. Lesson learnt for me in the future was follow one's instincts not somebody's well meaning advice that mostly has their own agendas mixed up in that advice. Unfortunately for me I entered a life of entrapment.

The family had rules, "what one sibling was given all others had to have as well". My 21st Birthday was approaching. As I had already left the family home, I thought I would be exempt from having the milestone party. But not to be. It was arranged by my family and was a wonderful event. It was a family reunion with my aunts and uncles in attendance. Also, I was to be given a symbolic watch as a present from my parents. I had a good watch that was given to me when I entered high school so didn't understand the need. So again, I followed orders and purchased the watch on behalf of my parents. One of my sisters stepped in and told me that my parents had spent a lot of money on my party and advised me not to ask for anymore money to cover the cost of the watch. So I paid for a watch that I really didn't need and couldn't afford.

When the date arrived for my party which was a two-hour drive away from Wagga to get there. I realised I did not know how I was going to travel there. I had met a young man briefly and the only person I knew that had a car so I asked him if he would take me. He made an excuse that his car would not be able to make the long drive. So being desperate I asked my friend's family to lend theirs as she was also coming with me, but neither of us had a driving licence. He agreed and we managed to attend without any problems.

My work filled my life and helped keep me in contact with the outside world. As Office Manager I worked long hours. A male worker employed under my instructions fresh out of school, lived at home with his parents, earned double my wage and could afford a car and things out of my reach financially.

I settled down to a manageable budget. Ate All Bran for breakfast. It soaks up the milk and leaves one feeling fuller in the stomach for longer. Also, good to keep one regular. A

Sandwich for lunch and Lambs Fry, gravy and vegetables for dinner. Lambs fry is cheap and full of iron. Smothered in onion gravy goes down well. Saturday afternoon I walked to a wholesale vegetable shop. The vegetables were straight from the farm. Was quite a hike but worth it. Got fit and ate well.

I settled into my life as it was. Not so homesick or feeling lonely. Just contented with my lot. I learned later that being with someone can make one feel lonelier than being contented in one's own company. Society tells us we are social animals and need human contact. That depends on the company. If it is not amicable it can be worse.

CHAPTER 3

My life was about to change for ever. I was a naïve 21 years old, and it was 1967. I did not know about mental illness and family dysfunction. Did not know about Psychopath, Sociopath or Frontal Lobe Brain injuries. These descriptions. Another one now added to the list is Narcissistic personally disorder. To me they have similar traits. Being disinhibition, loss of control of behaviour and emotions. Poor planning skills, lack of empathy, difficulty with seeing things from another person's perspective (self-centredness), personality changes, mood swings, uncontrollable anger which if not checked can result in physical harm and sometimes death of those closest to perpetrator.

A person with all these traits was about to come into my life. Being a kind hearted person with emphatic traits I was a sucker waiting to be caught. Coercive control is the label and Peter Pan was about to meet his Wendy. Stockholm syndrome would be the label I would be given. Society likes to judge us, but for me it became a survival mechanism which I invented as I went along.

I was leaving my place of employment and parked in front of the building was the young man that had kindly taken me to my 21st birthday party. I looked up and fortunately spotted his current girlfriend approaching. I continued onto my home wondering what that was all about. My workplace was out of the way of the general traffic. It was strange for these two to be going out of their way.

It wasn't long after that he started showing up at my place suffering from depression and suicidal thoughts. So, I became his councillor. Spent hours talking to him and eventually got him to remove the rifle he carried in his car. He was hard work and taking advantage of my kind nature.

I learnt from him the personality traits would have been inherited from his mother. She had the same issues which resulted in a pronounced upheaval in his life. His dad passed away suddenly at the age of fifty-six years. He was eleven years old at the time. His mum was violent and controlling. He mentioned to me a story when he was very young when his mum in a fit of temper bashed his head into the shed door and split his head open. She gave him lollies and made him promise not to tell his dad. I could imagine when his dad died and left him at the vulnerable age of eleven years without protection from his mother's outbursts would set off a traumatic insecurity. It also set off his Misogyny personality. Found it disturbing myself at family gatherings when they all appeared to take pleasure in other people misfortunes. It was hilarious and great entertainment for them.

His mum loved an audience, and I witnessed a few occasions when she showed off her need to be noticed. To be the centre of attention she made fun of her second husband in front of her friends. She degraded him about their sex life. One way of birth control or maybe avoiding any chance of intimacy. She also had a sharp tongue. Her behaviour was both physical and mental control.

Are we born with this need to control and disrupt the people close to us? I do know these people are very intelligent. I allowed myself to be trapped. Things that set him off were if I showed happiness, he would put me down. If I showed neediness, he would get angry. I became another person, not the one I wanted to be just to please him and keep peace. I was told by a friend of his family that the father that passed away had said the same thing about his mother. He married her because he had young children to raise. He had a successful business set up by his first wife who had a good knowledge of business. When he remarried his second wife, she demanded a housekeeper so that she could have trips to Sydney to visit her sisters. The older children had to help in the shop and look after their younger half siblings. He had to ask his son at the age of sixteen years to leave the family home because the wife did not get on with his son.

Our friendship continued with all it's ups and downs. The mood swings ever present and noticeable. He wanted to travel after his apprenticeship was completed. I was happy to accompany him on his travels, but he wanted to be married before we started our travels together. Reluctantly I gave in, and we purchased an engagement ring which I had to pay for. He never could manage money. Living at home he was provided for with out having to work out a budget. Responsibility was not part of his inherited disposition. I delayed the announcement for nearly a year after the ring was purchased. I jumped in knowing the pit falls thinking maybe he will mature one day; most people do learn as they go along. I didn't know at the time that he would never reach the emotional intelligence of an adult male.

I set the date of the wedding six months after he finished his apprenticeship. He went to the South Coast to work in the fishing industry as an Abalone diver. I returned to my parents' home where I worked and saved money to buy a caravan for us to live in while we travelled. He did eventually join me in my hometown to work, the excuse being the inclement weather on the South Coast interrupted the ability to work.

I made my own wedding gown and tried to keep the budget as low as possible. I was he last one in the family to be married so it was more of a relief for my parents to be finally finished with the responsibility of raising children. The wedding was as lovely as my 21st birthday party being a gathering of a reunion of my parents' siblings. I got the usual negative comment from a sister about my flashy rings. The truth being for me was I disliked jewellery never wore it much. Jewellery was a symbolic gesture required for social acceptance.

We married on the Saturday and the next evening my new husband introduced me to his new interest, Pornography. In the form of a newspaper, which I believe could be purchased from any newsagency in a sealed paper bag. He had purchase black and white photographs of a large breasted female. There must have been a sales deal as there was about 20 photographs as well as the same on slides to be viewed with special equipment. He also gifted to me a jar of special cream to be rubbed on the breast to enlarge them. I guess his idea was to turn me into the image of the model in the photo. I joked about the rubbing exercise must help with enlarging the breast muscle. I was contented with my body image and body shaming was not going to work on me. It was like the treatment his mother projected onto her husband, my stepfather in law. He got angry with me and said "it was the biggest mistake of his life marrying me ". I advised him that this mistake can be fixed by going to the courthouse and getting the marriage annulled. I had to go to work the next day, but he was not committed to a job at the time. I suggested he go to his mother's place for awhile until he sorts himself out. He was waiting for me when I got home from work on the Monday and no more was mentioned of his financial investment into what a female should look like.

A friend of my husband had spent a holiday in Cairns, and she spoke of how good it was, so that was to be the first stop on our travels. We arrived after the wet season had finished and settled into work straight away. I managed to get work with the same company I worked for in Wagga. My husband joined the Spear fishing club and made friends with the locals. One of these members had travelled following the spear fishing tourist attractions. So, Perth was to be the next stop of our travels. We stopped in at Wagga on our way to Perth, spending Christmas there.

Crossing the Nullarbor in the middle of summer was not fun but we made the most of this vast desolate countryside. We travelled mainly at night and spent the days out of the hot sun sitting in a small town's pub. At this time the Nullarbor was not a sealed road and we had three hundred kilometres of bull dust riddled road surface. The dust went through the car and caravan covering us in dust. Our hair and clothing were covered in dust and it was great to arrive at Eucla and have a shower even though it was sea water only available to clean with.

We obtained work immediately on arrival in Perth. I worked for Bunnings which was established in Perth in 1886 by two brothers who emigrated from England. In 1970 it was a thriving business but was to move on in the 1990s to what it is today. The business was immaculately kept. The large canteen that catered for the staff was the best I have seen in my years of working. My husband worked as a glazier for a while before moving on to caravan building.

CHAPTER 4

I became pregnant and we moved back to Wagga for the birth of the baby with intensions of eventually moving back to Cairns. We both got work immediately on our return to Wagga. My husband in building and myself in an office of a financial business. I worked up until my due date according to the doctor, but I had a different date for myself. Three weeks after his.

I was booked into hospital on the 21st ^{of} December for an induction to bring on labour. The doctor wanted the birth out of the way before Christmas, New year celebrations. Being young and naïve I did not see this as a violation of female's rights to have a comfortable natural birth. Being a first baby, the labour didn't progress as planned and I was heavily drugged for the night. In the morning an elderly Female Nurse came and sat with me. She did not examine me but just sat by my side and told me to shut my moaning up. She was a nurse from the second world war so I can understand why she seen me as a weakling. I was still under the influence of the drug given to me the night before and the only way of communicating was a moan. For some reason my brain did not connect to allow me to use words. Eventually the mid wife that attended me the day before arrived. She examined me and was horrified at the neglect.

I had a full bladder, and the baby was pressing on it making me feel very uncomfortable. A catheter was inserted, and the bladder emptied making room for the labour to continue. The doctor came just before lunch time to check on me. The mid wife promised that this baby would be delivered before he returned from his lunch break.

The birth went ahead quickly and naturally with her wonderful expertise help. The doctor got there in time to claim his involvement in the birth event.

My son had some trouble gripping the nipple to suck. My mother discovered the problem. The skin under the tongue was holding his tongue down. Old fashioned name Tongue Tied. I took my son for his check up and pointed the issue out to the doctor. He fobbed it off as unimportant but did snip the skin to free up the tongue. Also mentioned the issue to the child craft nurse on my next visit. In past visits she blamed me for being inexperienced. When I pointed out the problem and that it should have been picked up by an expert before I left the hospital. She got defensive and I never went back to the clinic. Worked it out for myself. Females at this time were treated as lower intelligent humans even by other females.

Not sure if the practice of not allowing the husband to be present at the birth sets off a trauma between couples. But in the 1970's hospitals had different practices. Some allowing family to be present and others not. My husband wanted to be present, but this hospital was adamant about not allowing him to be involved.

The abuse to me during birth may not have happened if a carer was present. Thank goodness it is now encouraged to have a family involved.

What followed on from the birth was the start of my life beginning to unravel. Bit like the quote of the frog starting out in cold water and the water slowly heating up and it's not sure when the water is too hot to escape.

I had to spend 10 days in hospital after the birth. This was the general practice of most post-natal care.

I was discharged on New years eve. There was a gathering of my husband's family at his parents' house. For reasons I was to discover later. My husband had purchased a ring (think it was a symbolic eternity ring). He presented the ring to me in front of all his family. While giving it to me he had a strange, angry expression on his face. He told me that he hoped I appreciated it as it cost a lot of money. One of his sisters must have noticed the angry look as she said he really did buy it without any pressure from family. I accepted it graciously. But what followed from that event left me totally confused and the ring became a symbol of betrayal.

We were still living in the caravan on a caravan park situated near Wagga. Not long after settling back in with my son a man knocked on the door of the van. Not recognising him I called to my husband to speak with him. They went outside to have a conversation. The next day the owner of the park came to see me, she had received a phone call from a woman that had left a phone number for me to call. I went to the phone box close by and rang the number. At first, I did not understand what she was saying. The penny dropped when she mentioned to me not to be coy about it as this was the first time she had been involved in this sort of thing. I hung up and when my husband came home, I told him about the phone call and gave him the number to call. My first mistake should have torn up the phone number and ignored it all. I was not as practiced in deceiving as my husband. In my absence he had reacquainted himself with his porno newspaper. Apart from selling products it advertised for couples who wanted to try sexual encounters. Probably to enhance their libido. For me I was married and happy with my libido. If I wasn't I would be still single and not breaking my marriage vows. The catholic religion allows Adultery by going to confession and all is forgiven. There is no consideration given to the upheaval of the family and the partner that has been betrayed.

My husband made the plans on my behalf to attend an evening meal with them at their house about a twenty-minute drive away. I made it clear I was not interested in disrupting my life for someone else's pleasure. I had just given birth and trying to establish a bond and breastfeeding with my baby.

I did attend the dinner with my tiny newborn baby in his bassinet. The lady allowed me to put him in her bedroom and explained she had five children. Another betrayal from a woman that should have known better. Was she been bullied into the practice by her husband. I didn't ask but there was no signs in the house of being any children ever present.

I flatly refused to be part of the life my husband had chosen and gave him permission to carry on with his life without me. He got angry of course, and I paid the price of a few bruises but not any broken bones. This was a better option than being raped by a stranger to please a group of psychopaths. To me these were people incapable of a loving intimate life. If I wanted that myself, I would never have entered a marriage. I had a newborn that needed security and the comfort of a mother's presence. I hated the dating scene and was longing to meet a suitable person to settle down with. Unfortunately, the man I thought was the one was seen as not suitable by my family. I will never know if it could have turned out differently if my family were accepting.

On the night that my husband was to meet up for his one-way swap, my son and I were taken to his mother's house to stay for the night. I guess I would not run away from there as he had completely fooled his mother with the gift of a ring. I would never tell her anyway. No mother wants to hear that their son is a perverted deviant. When he arrived home, he woke me up to give me a blow-by-blow description of his prowess in the bedroom with the couple. What a screwed up blithering idiot I was becoming. Started hating myself and lost all faith in humans including women most of all because I thought they were the glue that held society together.

About five months later I went to my parents 'home to house sit while they were away. My husband came and got me from my parent home, and I returned to the van with him. I got pregnant soon after and the decision was made to move to Cairns.

There was never any mention of the night with the couple again. But he did tell me something that happened in his childhood. The business ran by his parents was also their place of residence. It was Two doors from a pub. One evening there were two men and a lady very drunk coming from the pub. The threesome performed the act of sexual intercourse in front of the home with the parents watching and allowing this child to also witness. Obviously, my husband, being very young and impressionable, seen this as permission to grow up with the ambition to be just like them. If he was a normal child without a personality disorder, he would have grown up seeing the act as it really was. Not acceptable behaviour which leaves me to the opinion if I spoke to his mother would she believe me or think his behaviour was acceptable.

CHAPTER 5

Cairns has two different lifestyles. One being the wealthy tourists and the local population that live mostly in poverty. We rented a shed at the back of a wealthy couple's house. They also owned a cottage next door which was rented to a wealthy man in Sydney. The man from Sydney kept his concubine living there so that when he needed a break, she was there to help him out. She did landscape painting to pass the time. I settled down to a quiet life looking after my beautiful son. My son would get excited when my husband drove up after work, but he always got out of the car and went next door to visit this exciting woman with much more interesting things to talk about. My son would be disappointed he was stuck with his boring mother. My son was always escaping from the shed even though I locked the door he would get a chair and unlock the door to go for an adventure.

One day I got a visit from the exotic lady, she wanted cooking lessons on preparing fish. Her sugar daddy was bringing a business friend with him and she wanted to impress them with her cooking. My lessons must have been not up to scratch because she visited the next day to let me know the relationship had come to an end. She told me she envied my lifestyle and wanted to move back to New Zealand and her family. That helped me to feel good about myself. I was being true to what I wanted out of life.

The first New Year's Eve back in Cairns we attended a party held by my husband's friends. I was about six and half months pregnant. A lady approached me with something to say about my being pregnant and no wonder my husband was not interested in being with me. I gathered that he was giving her the hard luck story that married men give as a pickup line. We've all been given that old chestnut. Pathetic as it seems it does work on us sympatric types. My husband before we were married sucked me in with his depression and suicidal threats.

Two weeks later my husband had been out with his best mate at the time. His mate's wife was away at the time visiting her family for the summer break. Soon after they entered the home their intensions became apparent. My husband had decided with his friend to have sex with me. I call it rape as I was not going to allow this to happen. I put up a fight and being pregnant the man called off the rape. I went and hid until they left the home. The event was never discussed again. Just another trauma I buried to resurface later in life. I had dreams of being held down and panic attacks.

We moved from the shed to an old brick house in central Cairns. The house was owned by a couple that had a mechanical business next door. The house was cheap rent and would be condemned nowadays. Two plumbers were living there as well. They had put in a hot water system to make the place more liveable. The toilet was a pan in an outside building. The pan was picked up once a week by a council worker. Had to shoo the cane toads off at night before using it. The house was filthy so had to get down on my hands and knees to scrub the floors. Didn't have money for cleaning implements. Cashed in my life assurance to buy a fridge. The house was furnished with a two-burner gas ring, table and bench seat and beds that had bed bugs in the mattress. The bed bugs enjoyed making a feast on my pregnant belly.

I attended a local maternity clinic for my check ups and when the time came for the birth, I was attended by two mid wives. Because the baby was not putting on enough weight before the birth there was discussions of inducing me, but I had learnt my lesson and refused. I delivered a beautiful healthy daughter. She gained weight rapidly and slept well. Took her to the baby clinic regularly.

I had to wash by hand at this time but there was a lovely couple living next door and they took pity on me and gave me their old washing machine because they had replaced theirs. It was in excellent condition. Little gestures like this did restore my faith in humanity. Got to learn to swing with the good and the bad. My son was still the escape artist and I spent much of my time chasing after him to bring him back home. Taking him shopping was a nightmare, so I spent a lot of time at the local Botanic gardens with the children.

The window of opportunity opened for me to take a break from my marriage and living in the tropical heat of Cairns. I dislike humidity even though most of the population of the world live around this type of climate it isn't for me. Norther European countries usually are voted as the most liveable in the world. They are a cooler climate and smaller populations leading to a better and manageable lifestyle.

My husband and his friends, one being a pilot organised a trip to Tasmania. They were hiring the plane and going to spend the night break in Wagga with his parents. The pilot was not qualified for night flying. The arrangement was my son would travel with his father in the light plane to Wagga and I would nurse my daughter on a commercial flight from Cairns to Wagga.

My parents picked myself and children up from Wagga and drove us to their home. It was early January, and I quickly got a nightshift seasonal position with the local canary. I needed to replenish the bank account. I had taken out a bank account in joint names as I thought that is what a marriage should be based on. Working together to finance a home and maintain a family. My husband returned to Cairns after his holiday in Tasmania. The first week on his return I received a letter from him telling me he had been invited to a friend's birthday party. He was bragging about his meeting up with a lady and the affair that followed. Another blow to me but I should have known as he would have been lonely. The only issue for me it would have been great if he would just give me my freedom to get on with my life. I feared his angry uncontrollable outbursts and at times feared for my life. I was safe now but was never sure if I pushed too hard it would end in disaster.

CHAPTER 6

I took full responsibility of keeping my parents' home clean and did all the cooking. My children were fed, bathed and dressed for bed before I left for work. All my parents had to do was put them to bed. I would be home the next day when they woke up. I would have been working for about nine weeks before my sister-in-law intervened. She told me I was upsetting my mother and had to remove myself and children from her home. My father suggested I give my daughter to one of my sisters as she had two sons and could care for another. What my father didn't know she was contented with just two children. Her husband supported her financially and emotionally and her social life did not include adopting a one-year-old toddler. This behaviour toward single mothers that do not have financial support from the father is a disgrace. Children should not be removed from a mother that is willing to work. They should be supported by helping to keep the children safe while they bring in an income to put a roof over their heads and food on the table.

I had no alternative but to return to Cairns and an unsafe life. I wrote to my husband giving him our time of arrival. His main issue was his lover was returning from Brisbane and might be on the same flight.

I did find out eventually what happened with the affair. She got pregnant and had been in Brisbane for an abortion. She had two teenage daughters and from what my husband told me he was jealous of the attention she gave them. So, my chance of getting a quick divorce so they could marry did not happen. She was asking for more money from him as she had gone a shopping spree while in Brisbane and was short of cash. Her husband had left her to join the Merchant Navy but did leave her the car and the home to live in with her children. Her sister from Melbourne gave her the opportunity to go live in Melbourne with her. She came to the house to say goodbye to my husband. I had the children in the bath when she arrived, but my husband wouldn't answer the door, so I had to. Not sure what the conversation between them was about as I left them to it while I attended to the children.

About the same time as this was going on we visited my husband's friend's family-owned Resort. Was some sort of celebration as there was a lot of people in attendance. The stepfather of the friend, being a man in his seventies and had been drinking all day and very much under the influence of alcohol got upset by my husband's Narcistic behaviour. He entered the area where we were all gathered with a loaded double barrel shotgun with the intension of shooting my husband. Someone disarmed him and I missed out on another opportunity of becoming free.

I managed to get work in Cairns with my children in day-care, it left me free to settle into a day job. I was working at a Prawn Processing Plant. Peeling prawns that were then frozen into kilo size trays before being packed into cardboard packets the next day ready for sale. Out of the three hundred women that started the season I was one of sixteen remaining until the end of the season.

Most of the workers were Islanders. Beautiful natured women. I was given the job of lifting the heavy trays into and from the refrigerators. These were long metal containers that weighed a lot and to reach up to the top shelves took a lot of energy. But I was desperate to do well and provide for my children. After the wet season and the prawn processing centre closed the Abattoir opened for the dry season. The rules were to get a job one had to be a union member. So, I joined up and started working as a meat packer. The money was good. The only problem was going from the chilled boning room to the outside heat. I got an infection in my sinuses. Very painful, but as I discovered later on, is not as painful as tropical ear. My poor children got it first and when I succumb to it, I understood what the poor kids were going through. Most pain I have ever endured in my lifetime.

My daughter got seriously ill during this time. The tropics is a breeding ground for all sorts of exotic diseases that I was not equipped to handle. She had a bad chest infection and admitted to the Cairns Base Hospital where they discovered she had a parasite in her body causing her pneumonia. This was common in the soldiers during the second world war that were stationed in this area. After the diagnoses I was allowed to take her home and administer the tablets myself. Not an easy process trying to get a one-year-old to swallow a nasty tasting tablet.

During her two weeks stay in hospital I got to know the other mothers. Mostly Islander and Indigenous women. Some did not have the opportunity to take their children home, which was sad, but they handled it well. Beautiful souls. This was a similar situation when I had delivered my daughter in the Cairns Base Hospital. I was in a six-bed ward with Indigenous Ladies.

My daughter got her health back and I continued with work getting a nightshift waitressing job after the Abattoir closed. My husband needed a new car, so he went ahead and purchased a Mazda 4 sportscar. I was able to pay that off quickly as we were still living in the old house with cheap rent.

The gambling habit started off as a friendly Friday night out at mate's homes. As more people got involved it became serious. The drunker my husband and his mate got the more they would lose. The mate's wife and I would have to jump in and win enough money back to get us through the week.

I hated those nights. These were people that were supposed to be friends of my husband. I would opt out sometimes, but my husband would take the children. He knew I wasn't going anywhere without them. He also dropped me and the kids off to stay with the wives of his friends while he went fishing. On one occasion my children went with other children for a walk on the beach and someone hunted my younger children away. I noticed them going in the wrong direction, my daughter always following her brother fell from a bridge without any safety rails into a stony ditch. I made the mistake of calling out to them but too late my daughter turned toward me and walked backwards over the side. When I got to her, she was winded and had a gash to her head. Called an ambulance and took her to have the wound stitched. I always felt guilty for my daughter's bad health that plagued her all her life. She died at the age of forty-eight of aggressive brain tumours. She had allergy problems and suffered from Bronchial Asthma.

I was slowly bringing my husband around to the idea of me leaving Cairns and returning to Wagga to live. He was contented with his new car and the freedom of a busy social life. The option to stay in Cairns while I left to pursue my own life in

Wagga was a gentle suggestion. I learnt quickly that before you argue with someone, ask yourself, is this person mentally mature enough to grasp the concept of different perspective, if not there is no point to argue. After some consideration he agreed, but he was coming with me. He did remind me that it was death until we do part, and it would be my death. The children came first with me, and their welfare was priority even though having a irresponsible father didn't help keep them feeling safe and secure.

CHAPTER 7

On our return to Wagga, we got jobs straight away and lived with his parents until we purchased our first home. This was the 1970's and women's wages were still not calculated into the amount a couple could borrow to purchase a house property. Females were still slaves to their male counterparts. It would be my wage that provided for the family. My husband seen that what he earned was his to do with as he pleases. The bank loan did not cover the cost of the property, so we took out a small loan from my parents. Property prices had doubled over the past two years and interest rates were running at 17%. I negotiated to pay my parents loan off at 10% interest, which was a gift, but I did manage to get the money back to them in a year.

We lived with his parents for probably six months. Did wear out the welcome but I managed to purchase furniture for our home and leave it in the warehouse until we could move into our house. The solicitor kept delaying the final hand over. The property was a divorce settlement and I guess it was difficult to agree on settlement.

In the beginning my mother-in-law criticised me for my affection and care shown to my children. In her day mothers had to inflict capital punishment as that toughened up the child. She didn't understand the concept of tolerance and compassion not weakness, rather they are strengths. I did not want my children to lack empathy but resilience to navigate this cruel world. While we were living there, she did see the results of how her son had turned out as a responsible adult. He was never there to help. He went from work to the pub and weekends with friends. The reality must have been a shock. But it was always about appearances and as long as it was hidden from others knowing it was okay. Bit like the English Royal Family.

My first job was at the private Calvary Hospital. Started the day doing admissions, then front desk and surgery theatre lists. In the afternoons was discharges of patients. My sister-in-law minded the children during my working hours. I was always home for them when I wasn't working. My mother-in-law made it clear she was not going to take care of the children while I worked. She married into an established business and stable Husband that provided well. I have heard women criticising other women for working. They did not understand that not all men could provide. Life gives us experiences that others cannot comprehend. The saying, judge not, that you be not judged. For with that judgement, you judge: and with the measure you use, it will be measured back to you.

Fortunately, a new meat works opened in the city, and I got a labouring job with them. Better pay and shorter hours. There was an early morning start that made it possible to have the children minded in the morning, but I was home when they finished school.

It was a struggle at first to cover the cost of repayments and keep food on the table. The kids and I missed meals occasionally as the bills had to be covered to keep the roof over our heads. Occasionally my husband would come home from the pub early with a bundle of fish and chips. He would sit at the kitchen bench and eat them in front of us. The look on my son's face was one of envy, he probably would love something different not just the basic foods I fed him. Fortunately, my children were still too young to see the blatant selfish act it was.

I always had to have a meal in the oven for when he did get home even if he had eaten elsewhere and the meal did not get eaten. Had to replace a lot of oven elements over the years. I did eventually get a microwave oven and he could reheat the meal when he chose to. The work I did was physically exhausting and by the end of the week I was flat out stringing a sentence together. One evening I had cooked lasagne. Served it up for us and left the remaining in the dish. Not thinking he was incapable of dishing it up for himself. About midnight he came home from the pub, pulled me out of bed to serve the meal and accused me of not respecting him enough to serve him a meal on a plate. I didn't do that again, no matter how tired I was it was always in the oven covered.

I envied the couples that shared their responsibility together, of working and their homelife. They spent their after-work time together doing, sharing the domestic duties. They could go to bed together and have a loving sex life. I was made fun of because I went straight home from work to my family on my own. I read to my children at bedtime and helped with their school homework. I was in reality a single mother.

My children missed out on opportunities that their father had been given when he was a child. Being born into wealth set up by a previous marriage of his father. My husband did not understand the struggles of building a life together as a young couple. He wasn't aware of financial responsibilities and was not capable of empathy. My children were teased and bullied because of the home-made clothing and grooming.

I enrolled them in swimming lessons, and they showed potential but when the indoor pool closed, I had to find something else for them to do. My daughter did gymnastics for a while through a private tutor which was a convenient bus ride from our home. Eventually she joined the PCYC which was set up for disadvantaged children. She did well. Winning medals for marching and floor gymnastics.

My son took an interest in computers, and I eventually I got him a Commodore computer and had the phone line installed so he could have dial up connection to the outside world. The problem being my husband would come home unexpectedly and want to use the phone. There would be a tantrum from my husband when that happened my son would have to stop what he was doing. We know why it's called dysfunctional families.

My son had developed learning problems. Picked up during a school medical check. He was short sighted which develops over time and is noticeable in early teens. He had special tutoring provided by the school, but it still set him back for the rest of his school life. He did get an early entrance in university to study and obtained a bachelor's degree. My daughter left home after year eleven to attend a academy in Sydney to do a certificate in Beauty Therapy. She worked while she studied, and I was able to be a back up for her financially. My husband gave up smoking inside the house the day she left to go to Sydney. She had Bronchial Asthma and the tobacco smoke set it off and she would have to spend the time in her bedroom when he was around.

My eldest brother and his wife would take the kids for a break on their farm to spend time with their cousins during the summer school holidays. It must have been a relief to get away from the dysfunctional environment and be in a safe home for a while. My daughter cried the first few days when she had to return to chaos. My husband would take us occasionally to the south coast for a weekend. This was probably out of having to appear a decent bloke rather than wanting to be around his family.

CHAPTER 8

Most of the time he spent his weekends at the pub or off on his outdoor activities with his best friends. He took his annual leave on long trips to the Norther Territory with a group of his mates. His friendships took priority over his family's needs. When my mother passed away, he could not attend the funeral. It coincided with duck opening weekend and he had arranged to be with his very best mate. He threw a tantrum and accused my father of arranging the funeral on the Saturday to interfere with his weekend. I was able to catch a bus to Leeton for the funeral and he picked me up on his way home from his weekend. I was disappointed in his attitude toward me as without the financial backing my parents gave us, we would not have been able to buy our home. This is typical behaviour of a mental unstable person.

I had paid off the loan to my parents and eventually saved enough money to pay off a lump sum on the bank loan. A clause in the agreement being a lump sum of $5,000.00 could be paid off the capital at any one time. The loan could be paid over thirty years but with interest it would have tripled the original loan value. This was achieved by my children not getting luxuries. We wore second hand clothing and ate just basic meals. Life was to school or work and home. There was no fancy take aways meals or nights out to the movies. Take away meals and holidays for the man of the house only. He did give up the gambling but maintained his heavy drinking and smoking and a busy social life. The publican and tobacconist did well out of him as would the taxation department. It is not fair that these items are so heavily taxed that the families of these addictive people must go without because the addiction takes priority.

I took it on the chin when I was criticised by my family or in laws. I probably appeared to be a blithering idiot because I didn't belong to a golf or tennis club. Didn't socialise, but I hid from them the truth of what was going on in my life. My mother-in law offered to have my children overnight while my husband and I went to a social dance night. She often looked after daughter's children while they had their night out together. We arrived at the hall where the function was being held. Immediately on arrival my husband disappeared. I sat in the corner by myself as I did not know anyone else there. A man did chat with me for a while. My husband made an appearance when it was time to go home. He had arranged for his best friend and his date to visit with us at home. On our arrival home it was explained to me that we were going to swap partners for the night. I flatly refused and locked myself in my son's bedroom. So, date night for me was going to be always a romp around with strangers not the romantic night I imagined should be. My husband would tell me we had nothing in common, I agreed so why didn't he do something about it. All he had to do was leave the house and get on with his life with the people he wanted to be around. Instead of moving on he would threaten me with violence if I ever left. He knew he couldn't manage without the stability I provided for him. As long as I played along with him, I would be safe.

I visited my parent's home twice a year on one of the long weekends. My mother had a stroke that paralysed the left side of her body. She was permanently disabled and in a wheelchair for seven years before she passed. They employed a carer that did basic housekeeping and caring for my mother. The heavier jobs were carried out by the rest of the family. I would visit and help with these jobs. My husband would drop me off at the railway station in a nearby town that would take me direct to Leeton. On arrival back on one particular weekend. I went about what had to be done to get me ready to return to work the next day. My children were about seven and eight years old and their bed linen was in a Disneyland print that was the fashion at the time. Went to put my daughter to bed and when I pulled the bed sheets back found a large bloody semen mess on the sheets. I had to act quickly to protect my seven-year-old from seeing the mess. Stripped the bed and remade it so that she could settle down for the night.

This was a double betrayal. It was disturbing that two adults could do this in a child's bed and pull up the bedding and walk away. My husband tried denying it was him. But by this time, I knew that he was a pathological liar. I recognised the body language of these types. Just imagine an eight-year-old trying to get out of something he knew he had done wrong but wasn't going to own up to it.

The reality for me was that if I walked away from the home, these were the people who would take over my house. I was the sole provider for myself and my children and if I up stumps and left it would be another financial burden. My kids were settled into school. I was a proud housekeeper and kept my home and garden in good condition.

I was learning quickly how to handle this type of behaviour, especially if my husband was sober. Being sober is when he is at his nastiest and most dangerous. Under the influence he would be slightly calmer, and I knew he would eventually pass out and I would be safe. His moods were hard to predict which left me pretending to be what he needed me to be. He got angry if I showed signs of happiness as this was only allowed when he was happy. He got angry when I showed signs of weakness or illness. He needed me to be in control of my emotions all the time.

Western medicine is so far behind in diagnosing these people and treating them in accordance with their requirements. Muslim religion does not allow alcohol consumption. Hopefully they have another way of treating their members to keep the domestic abuse under control. There has been an early childhood diagnosis of personality disorders introduced and hopefully with education the violence and upheaval these mentally ill, by the time they reach adulthood, can be reduced. There hasn't been any evidence yet, in the reduction of this type of behaviour.

I accepted my loveless marriage. I would never trust another person to allow them to enter my personal life. Single mothers attract Paedophile's as these types befriend the mother to get access to their children. That is why society must give women the tools to manage providing financially and emotionally for their children. We are gradually progressing to equal opportunities. We do not have to have a man sign on our behalf to get access to credit. We are allowed to own our own homes and make decisions without permission from a male. Some countries are a long way from allowing that to happen. I was fortunate as I was allowed to make my own financial decisions. Some people are coerced into allowing full control by their abusive spouse of what they earn. I guess I was locked into providing financially for family while my husband had freedom of his own income for his social image.

The meat works where I was working was closing it doors. Wasn't viable financially anymore. I did get a job for awhile working with the Department of Agriculture at the experimental farm. This was contracted for two years. When the contract came to an end, I was offered another position with the department in another town. Decided I did not want to disrupt my children's education and connection to community. So turned it down. During this time, I decided to have another child. Probably not the best decision but it was acceptable to bring children into the world without a proper father. Not sure my grown-up daughter would agree but I gave her the chance at a life now well lived by her. My mother-in-law was pleased saying it would strengthen our marriage. I envy the people who live in a fairy tale world not having to face reality on a daily need to survive. I protected both families, mine and his from the mental disorder he suffered. Society wasn't ready for the truth yet.

Being well into my thirties I was referred to a specialist for the pregnancy and post-natal care. Being fit and healthy I did not have any issues and delivered a healthy daughter. There was a nine-year gap between my daughter and new baby. My son became the babysitter, and the responsibility taught him to grow into a compassionate well adjusted adult man.

CHAPTER 9

My husband hadn't matured emotionally though and carried on with his busy social life. When my daughter was just a few weeks old there was to be a special celebration at the local pub for his best mate. Something to do with a football award. I was reluctant to go but being his special friend, he needed to keep up appearances and have his wife attend. I was treated the same as always. Seated at the bar while he disappeared to wherever he went at such events. I got some strange looks from the other bar dwellers with a newborn cradled on my lap. Who knows what was going on in their heads?

Six months later I had to attend at the same pub. His best friend was celebrating his engagement with a special gathering of family and friends of both couples. Of course, I had to attend for a different reason this time, he was showing off his new lover. So, the usual, left sitting on a bar stool with my six months old baby in my lap. Probably an hour later my husband made a spectacular appearance in front of me. He was down on his hands and knees with the lady sitting astraddle on his back. They stopped in front of me. All his friends cheered them. The party got underway. The women decided they all wanted a nurse of my baby. She was passed around like a rag doll.

The look of fear in her eyes was disturbing. Young children are aware of emotions in the adults around them. These adults were drunk, so would have been giving off unsettling vibes. On the way home from this outing my husband told me all about his new friend and the fact she had five children. Not sure if these children were neglected while she carried on at the pub or there was a responsible adult looking out for them. Pubs have been redesigned now to cater for families if one can afford to attend.

Six months later when my daughter was almost a year old the best friend was getting married. My husband was Groomsman and of course I had to be there for appearances sake. My children were being minded by family. I stayed long enough to appear to be part of the celebration. When the time came, I escaped and picked up the children and went on home. My husband's friends brought him home legless and put him to bed.

The next day was the after-wedding celebration barbeque. Husband's friends and wives arrived at my home for early morning get together before the lunch time cook up. The usual Aussie gathering, men in the shed and women in the kitchen. I wasn't very hospitable, and I paid the price later at the barbeque with lots of nasty remarks directed to me. These were the people that cheered in my presence during my husband's and lover's floor show six months previously. I hadn't forgotten, was reeling from the betrayal still. I was glad when it was all over, and I could go home and be by myself.

People think being alone makes you lonely, but I don't think that is true. Being surrounded by the wrong people is the loneliest feeling in the world.

I returned to work when my daughter was three and three quarters years old. My son was fourteen years and my daughter twelve years. The eldest two were now in high school and able to get themselves off to school in the morning and drop their little sister off at the babysitter.

The local meatworks had just reopened with a new owner. I did a labours job for the first few months. These were the jobs that were allocated to women. Lower income and longer hours. I asked about being trained into a position that had better pay and shorter hours. These were jobs given to men. I still hear the accusations made by both females and males about women taking men's jobs. Does that mean that women should live in poverty because the man they are married to will not provide for them and their children. After much arguing I was given the chance to better myself. Being female, I had to be better at the job than my male counterparts and not to take time off from my job if my children were ill. Men were allowed as much time off as they wished but woe if a woman needed to take time out for her children or herself. This practice was a reason for not giving women these types of jobs. I worked hard and became skilful with the use of a knife and opened the door to other women following in my footsteps. This type of work is now given to refugees that arrive in Australia to seek safety from a country too dangerous to live in.

I was now doubling my husband's pay before tax and starting a superannuation fund. I decided to make some improvements in my life. The first one being a new bed. Unfortunately, I went ahead and bought it without getting permission from my husband. He sulked for a week and refused to sleep in the bed. He slept in a lounge chair. After the week was up and his little tantrum proved a point, he had his first night's sleep in the new bed. Turns out it was the best most comfortable bed he had slept in. It was the best weeks sleep I had ever had without a drunken snorer beside me.

After that was the installation of the telephone so my son could access the internet. I did get permission this time and all was good.

I decided to take my children shopping for school uniforms. No more shabby old ones anymore. We entered the uniform shop together. So I thought, but on looking around to check, my youngest was not following us. I rushed outside to get her, but she had disappeared. I hit the panic button and as one does in a panic, I did a stupid thing. I went to the pub where my husband hung out to let him know. He turned his back on me and pretended he did not know me. The pub was near the police station, so I went there, and she was perched up at the desk happily playing. Some do-gooders must of picked her up quickly and took her to the station. Usually when I am out in a public area, and I spot a child that looks lost I watch to make sure they are safe until the parent arrives to collect them. Sometimes do-gooders take action that creates chaos in other people's lives. Do they do that to make themselves feel good at the cost of others? My husband told me on his arrival home after the pub incident "to never make a fool of him in public again". Yep he is definitely a Narcissist.

In the late 1980's we were now debt free, and my job was bringing in a decent income. I was ready to let go of the family home and move onto buying a house with the family home as collateral. The home was in joint names. I understand and respect that men need to be in control of all decisions in a relationship. At least appear to be. The real estate was at this time a buyers' market. I started research into buying property. Women were given the excuse that they could not take out a mortgage because they may get pregnant and not be able to work. I had remedied that problem by having a tubal ligation after my third child was born.

I let my husband know what my intensions were. He could get on with his life and bring home as many randoms as he needed without disruptions. He kept telling me we had nothing in common. I was always going to be true to myself and pig headedly going to live my life the way I wanted. He told me I was going to end up a lonely old woman. He had managed to skew with my mind enough to turn me into a distrusting loaner. I could live with that if I was free from abuse. He also made fun of me telling me that houses weren't just picked up off shelves like at a supermarket. Better to tell a female she is too dumb to decide for herself.

So, he decided he wanted to redeem himself and buy a block of land, design and build a house on it. He said it was in honour of my hard work. I thought about that and decided it was a good financial move. We had to borrow some money to cover the cost of the land. My husband didn't want to borrow from a bank and asked me to ask my parents for a loan. At this time my mother was terminally ill. I mentioned that to my husband, but he was adamant, so I went ahead and asked, but my parents declined. We took out a loan with a solicitors' firm that dealt in family Trust Funds. The solicitor was quite surprised to be doing business with a female. It took a decade to eventually build on the land.

The police were clamping down on drink driving so it was becoming difficult for my husband to have his social outings at his pub. So, he began his social rounds drinking at friends' homes. He started brewing his own beer and that was a big financial saving. I find it disturbing that a lot of this country's revenue is raised by taxing addictive products. We are told it's a deterrent to people not starting on these products. If this is so, why isn't there an alternative offered up to those that have become addicted. Families live in poverty because they must provide for their addiction. These people are paying more tax than their wealthy counterparts.

My husband was a perfectionist at his work as a builder. He was well known for his knowledge of the industry. He was working at a joinery shop teaching young apprentices the trade when he was terminated from the company. There was a public known reason, but he confessed to me the real reason. The young apprentices were in their mid-teens and at an impressionable age. According to my husband he wanted to impress these young men by bragging about his extra marital affairs. One of the young men asked why he treated his wife so badly. I cannot print what he told me he had said about me, it was disgusting and inappropriate. The responsibility of the owners of the business to these apprentices and the parents of these lads was being undermined by my husband. Society is not going to move forward to giving females respect while it has men like him. He was in his late forties so never going to change but he did move onto other jobs and treat his colleagues with respect.

CHAPTER 10

In the late 1990's we had paid off the block of land that we had purchased in joint names. I had my driving licence for just under 10 years and I purchased a new car. Both of my parents were deceased. My son was now living and working in Sydney and eldest daughter living and working in London England. My youngest daughter had just about completed her high school years. I had shouted myself, my son and daughter on a tour through Tasmania. I was emotionally separated from my husband. Did not expect any acknowledgment from him so would not result in disappointment on my behalf. He still considered his friends priority in his life. He had lots of camping, fishing, shooting trips with his mates. His holidays away, were planned around them. I provided the stability for him at home. This is what a childlike mentality required. I called it the royalty syndrome. The world revolved around him and if anyone wanted to take that away from him off with their head.

This newfound freedom for me must have triggered a need for my husband to start building his long- time plan to build his forever house. The building started in January 1998. My husband wanted to keep our house we were living in and rent it out. I talked him out of the idea, as deep down I knew that he was incapable of taking responsibility of the management of a rental. The house was sold three days after putting it up for sale, so we had to find a rental for ourselves while the new dwelling was completed enough to live in. We had to borrow a small amount of money to complete it after we had moved in.

After settling into the new house built on ten acres of land my husband became happier with himself. In his mind he had redeemed himself. He still had manic mood swings, but the alcohol kept him calm. I spent as much time at work as I could as it was much better than being at home. In the winter of 2007, my husband had a massive heart attack and almost did not survive it. He had a quadruple bypass in St Vincent's hospital and made a complete recovery. He continued to abuse his body with tobacco and alcohol but in smaller quantities. His friends now considered him as " too much work" and did not associate with him anymore. I had to now look after him without any break from his neediness. With this new reality I got angry. This person that put everybody else before he even considered his family was totally dependant on us. In his decline I asked if there was a lady friend I could invite to visit. He replied with "they are long gone". What a shame that this man was now relying on his wife that he abused mentally and physically for nearly fifties years. To me he was a child in a man's body. I wonder how his friends both male and female conceived him to be. Did he fool them with his social charms, or did they occasionally see him for what he truly was.

I retired in 2012 feeling burnt out so spent a year relaxing then my husband retired so I took up volunteer work three days a week. I enjoyed the volunteer work as it gave me a release from home life without any pressure that a paying job has. I planned a holiday for my seventieth birthday. This was through Northern Territory and North-western Australia. These were the places my husband visited with his mates every second year. I was to be away for three weeks. I did not want to impose on my children to look after their father, so I took him with me. He was a handful, and on my return from the holiday I was so stressed from lack of sleep I had a mental breakdown.

There wasn't any help available for me at that time, so I just got on with it and sorted myself out by myself. Two of my siblings would call me from time to time and when I mentioned my problem, they would say "aren't you over that yet". It's amazing as they both said the exact same words to me on different occasions. I guess it was their way of saying wake up to yourself which was probably what I needed to do.

There isn't a rule book to follow to help us manoeuvre through our life's journey. It's just muddle along as best we can. Much harder when the person you should be able to rely on the most is mentally ill and revels in disruptive behaviour.

For me it was to keep myself and my children on an even keel. It's easier to stay with a dangerous person if you are cleverer enough to tame their toxic behaviour. It's harder to walk away not knowing if you are safe. Maintaining a comfortable lifestyle for yourself and children is priority.

I was lucky I had three beautiful natured children. They didn't inherit the antisocial personality disorder gene. My husband had inherited this from his mum as she demonstrated the same symptoms as my husband.

My son went on to live a normal life. He was taken on camping, fishing and duck shooting trips by his father from about the age of twelve years. These camping in the bush lessons taught him to be resilient with survival instincts that a lot of boys miss out on.

Probably the most disturbing practice was when it came time to go home his dad would need to catch up at his local pub. My son was left roaming the street while he waited for his dad to take him home. My husband never offered him to accompany him or give him money to buy himself a meal and drink at the local take way cafes. My husband was a selfish person with never any consideration to how another human may be feeling.

CHAPTER 11

My son met his future wife during his university years. She and her sister were doing similar degrees to him. She and her family were refugees from Vietnam. Displaced from their country because of a war. Her father worked for the Old Regime" (Republic of Vietnam). After the war he was called to enter re-education camp. But it was a form of penal servitude. He entered the camp on the 24 June 1975 and was released by the communist party on 7 July 1981. During this time her father's health declined and he had poor eyesight. Her mum had to provide food for her husband and travelled days on a train to get food to him over these years he was imprisoned.

After her dad's release they planned their escape from the brutal inhuman treatment of the new communist's regime. It cost a lot of money to make the journey from Vietnam to safety in Thailand. On the way to escaping her mum and two sisters were arrested and were left behind in Saigon under the ever-watchful eye of government officials.

Her father, sister, brother and herself boarded a boat along with fourteen other people. They started the journey to Thailand on the 31 January 1982 and arrived 26 February 1982. The motor gave out in the middle of the ocean, and they drifted for eleven days before being rescued. They ran out of food and water but survived. Many did not arrive to safe shores.

The refugee camp was more like a prison. Thirty-one months without seeing the outside world. During this time the children attended school and worked hard at their lessons.

They were eventually accepted by the Australian Embassy and were moved to another camp which is called "transit camp". In this centre they went through a program called "Australian Orientation Program" (A.O.P.) They learnt to speak English and the lifestyle in Australia. They arrived in Sydney 12 September 1984. After spending two weeks in Sydney in a hostel they flew to Wagga 25 September 1984

The Uniting Church Wagga Congregation paid the airfares and set them up in accommodation and obtained employment for the father. The two sisters and son were enrolled into school. As soon as they arrived in Australia her dad started the process of getting his wife and two other daughters out of Vietnam. After six years of being separated they were all finally united on the 20 June 1990 with all the family settling in Wagga before moving to Sydney to be closer to the Vietnamese community. In the six years of waiting for them they received many letters that they were coming to Australia. Unfortunately, the Vietnamese Government would keep stalling and after much negotiation they were let go to finally reconcile as a family in Australia.

The daughters remained in Wagga to finish their university degrees. The youngest a son could not speak Vietnamese so communication with his mum was limited for a while.

When my future daughter in law's dad discovered his daughter was in a relationship, with my son he ordered his daughter back to Sydney to live with them. The father wanted to see his daughters married to Vietnamese men.

This broke my son's heart. We shed a few tears over the unfairness of having the connection broken. A close friend of the family and member of the Uniting Church intervened and helped to enable them to communicate with each other again. My son made many visits to Sydney to meet up with her, eventually he moved to Sydney permanently. He had saved up a good deposit on a one-bedroom unit in Mascot where they lived after their marriage.

They eventually fronted the father about them getting married. Because they both had waited so long to get permission to marry, the father gave in, and the engagement was announced. They married at the end of 1999. We had the traditional Vietnamese Ceremony at the parent's house with an alter set up for the occasion then onto the Civil Ceremony held in the gardens of the apartment complex where my son lived.

There was a large gathering of the Vietnamese Community on the Sunday evening following the wedding. The traditional dress was worn by the women which gave a colourful atmosphere to the event.

My daughter-in-law and the eldest sister purchased and paid for the family home for their parents to live in. Their eldest a daughter was born in 2008 and the son born at home a few years later. The home birth was not planned to be that way. My daughter in law was to finish work the next day but her son had other plans and my son delivered him at home. The Ambulance took them to the nearest Hospital.

My son and his wife have a successful marriage, both working hard to set themselves up financially and provide well both financially and emotionally for their two children. My son's wife also volunteers her time to working in the community to improve the social lives of others.

They both had disruptive childhoods, but both have dealt with this set back amazingly well. Just got on with their lives without any animosity to those hard times. I am very proud of their achievements. My life was well spent when this is the outcome of my efforts.

CHAPTER 12

My second child a daughter was born fifteen months after my son was born. She was a contented baby and gained weight rapidly. I was able to bond and establish breast feeding without any disruptive behaviour in my marriage at that time. She was born in Cairns, and I did not have the knowledge of the pitfalls of living in the tropics. We lived in poverty as it takes a lot of money to survive in the tropical areas.

She did well at school and was a high achiever both academically and in the sports arena. My children just accepted the fact that they had one responsible parent. Even so my daughter did crave for acceptance and acknowledgement of her achievements by her father. He was not capable of being a responsible, caring adult.

She worked part time from the age of fourteen years to support herself and took on the responsibility of getting on with what ever needed to be done. She wanted to move to Sydney to further her studies at the end of year ten, but I persuaded her to stay on for another year to mature a little more. At the age of sixteen years, she moved to Sydney and completed her chosen career course. She commenced work in Sydney for a while but moved back to Wagga to save up to travel. She did not live with me but shared rent with other people.

She saved enough to travel by herself to meet up with a Contiki tour to travel around Europe. After the Contiki tour ended she continued her travels with several young ladies she had met on the tour. They visited the countries that were not included in their Contiki adventure. Eventually she settled in London for two years on a working visa. She started working in a bar like most Australian travellers in London. She was given the responsibility of helping run the kitchen, cooking and serving pub meals. She was noticed and offered a job by a Chiropractor doing therapy massage.

She shared accommodation with some local people she had met through her job. She returned to Australia with one of these friends and they travelled and worked along the East Coast of Australia until his working visa ran out and he returned to England.

On her return she worked for a few years in Sydney before coming back to Wagga to save to return to London England. Living back in England she met up with the man that was to be the father of her son. He was going to accompany her to Australia for the birth, but he changed his mind and she returned to live with me for the birth of her son.

Three years after the birth she decided to apply for a university degree as a mature student. She was accepted and went on to do well, winning scholarships and several publications in research. I provided the support for her as she was able to live with me and we shared the responsibility of her son my grandson. She never received any financial support from the father of her son.

With the hard work and effort, she was able to buy a new car and pay off a block of land. She designed the home she wanted to build on the block with the help of her father. He finally at the age of seventy years gave her the attention and recognition she deserved. He passed away a year before the building of her house commenced. She was in a relationship at this time, but they did not live together choosing to meet up at his house. She remained living with me to give her son the security of the home he was born into. It was close to his school and the university where she worked.

Her dad passed away twelve months before she was to begin the build of her house so she took on the full responsibility of working with a local builder to achieve her own home. Two months after the construction started, I got a phone call from my grandson saying his mum had arrived at the school to pick him up, but she was not well. I arrived at the school and sat with her in her car while the ambulance arrived. She kept having epileptic seizures. Being Friday afternoon, it took ages for the Ambulance. It took a long time to stabilise her before transporting.

Eventually it was established that she had three brain tumours. She was admitted to St Vincent's hospital in Sydney where she had a biopsy taken of the tumours and radiotherapy given while her head was open. The result of the biopsy was a shock to both my daughter and her partner of only a few years. The tumours were aggressive, and she was given a diagnosis of six months. She fought hard and when the radiotherapy was ceased, she went onto to chemotherapy which extended her life for another twelve months. Her partner took her to her many appointments in Sydney and in the meantime we all chipped in and got her house built.

She moved into her home and lived there for three seasons. She celebrated her 48th birthday the night before going into a coma and entering palliative treatment for end-of-life care.

Her son was in year ten at the time of her diagnosis. He remained living with me so that there was less upheaval in his day-to-day life. He eventually moved into his mum's house halfway through year eleven where he stayed until he went off to Canberra for university. I stayed with him in his home during his year twelve school days so that he could maintain his focus on exams. During year eleven he worked part time at Coles filling home delivery orders. I was able to assist him to get his driving license which he got first try. He achieved high marks during his high school years and received early acceptance to ANU.

It is the greatest reward when children work hard to achieve and be the best they can be. His mum would be very proud of him. She did well to raise a beautiful son without any help apart from myself.

CHAPTER 13

My third child a daughter was born early 1980's. Her brother was 10 years old and her sister 9 years. She was a gentle soul, unlike her older siblings. She struggled with understanding the dynamics of the family she was born into. I was either working or distracted with keeping the home tidy and clean. I was still the main supporting parent which I hid from my children. They did not know my story as I kept my secret to myself. The acceptance of divorce in the 1980's was now an alternative to living in disharmony. A lot of my daughter's friends' parents were in their second or third marriage.

With teenage children now, my husband changed his physical abuse to coercion. Gone were the days of bruised ribs that were especially difficult when the children were toddlers and had to be lifted. He had to keep up appearance in front of his two children who were old enough now to work things out for themselves.

I was now the perfectly trained wife. I earned enough to provide well for us all without my husband having to feel underprivileged. This tactical genius had everyone under his spell of being the perfect father and husband. He would drive past my daughter on the way home from work at the same time as she finished school. It could be pouring rain and he would give her a wave on the way past, not giving it a thought of how she would appreciate a gesture of a lift out of the rain.

Kind gestures go a long way to making us feel good about society but my husband saved them for strangers or friends so he could keep up outside appearances. He had a doting dad up until he was eleven years old and even though his mum was physically violent toward him, she did give him attention.

Being ignored by a father and not knowing why, would have set off feelings of self-doubt on my daughters' behalf. Parents are supposed to give unconditional love. My heart had been broken enough by this man, so I ignored his bad behaviour, but my daughter was not old enough to figure it out yet. She suffered from low self-esteem and disillusioned with his ignoring her.

She got a part time job and left home at the age of fifteen years. I kept in touch with her, and we maintained a mother daughter connection. Daughters need a good father figure in their lives not a nasty, chaotic, confusing parent.

She settled into a relationship, and they had three children together before eventually having the courage to get married. Was a beautiful civil ceremony in the gardens of a restaurant with lots of their friends in attendance. She worked and helped raise their children while obtaining a university degree in Social Welfare. Her job is very rewarding as she helps people to sort out their problems when life sends them difficult times.

She shares the responsibility fairly with her husband as a marriage should be. The children are given the opportunities that my daughter missed out on because she was raised by a single mother. She would not have been aware of the situation during her childhood days because I hid the truth for my own protection.

I was born to parents that were burnt out from having children. Being number eight of nine I had lots of older siblings and their spouses. Growing up I was constantly reminded to not upset my mother and not to ask for assistance if I found a process too difficult for my young age. I became capable at an early age to do most things by myself. I taught myself to read and write before I started school as I thought that was what was required, I believed that if I could not manage a chore by myself, I was not to ask for help.

When I was given advice by an older sibling or sibling's partners, I took it on board and believed it without questioning it. I know now not to listen to peoples 'advice as they have their own agendas. One must follow their own instincts and believe in themselves.

I did manage to make myself heard occasionally and not have to participate in some of life's milestone events. I refused confirmation of my Baptism, refused to make my debut. I regretted accepting to have a 21st Birthday party and getting married. These were not part of what life for me was all about.

I did not have to adorn myself with jewellery, never wore makeup. Being well groomed, clean and sensible comfortable clothing was necessary. The rest is a waste of money. I never had any desire to fit in. No plans to walk with the crowd. I had my own mind and soul. But it took me years to realise how important that was to me.

During my High School years, females were checked on the length of their school tunics. Sports tunics were measured by kneeling on the floor and the hem had to reach the floor to be an acceptable length.

I was about 15 years old and was to compete in a combined High School Athletics Carnival representing my School in Long Jump or Triple Jump. This required a long run up and leaping into a sand pit. During the event a group of boys the same age as myself laid on their stomachs at the end of the pit so they could look up our skirts while we jumped. They made commentary of what they could see up our tunics as we finished the jump and exited the sand pit.

This was accepted behaviour by the teachers and judges as the boys were ignored by them. Intelligent Males and Females would see the disrespect of that type of behaviour and call it out for what it was even in those days of accepted misogynistic behaviour.

It was in the 1980's that the Education Department wanted to introduce Education to improve the knowledge of Pre-Pubescent boys and girls on personal development.

During this time, I would walk my two eldest children to school with my youngest in the stroller. Lady who lived in a house that I passed by each day would be standing at her gate and say hello.

She invited me and my daughter to morning tea, so I decided to meet up with her at our convenience one morning after dropping my children off. She told me about being lonely and that she was forbidden by her husband to read magazines or newspapers. He didn't like her having contact with the outside world.

She believed she was mentally ill and with her husband's permission she entered a mental facility to be assessed. The diagnosis for her was she was normal and the problem was her husband's treatment of her. She mentioned she would contact her father who lived in Victoria to get advice. I lost contact with her when I returned to work.

Her husband was an active and well-respected member of The Catholic Church. He was an instigator in setting up a partition to block the Personal Development Education Programme in Schools. He knocked on my door one day to have me sign the partition, knowing what he was personally I was shocked. I did not agree to blocking our children's advancement into developing into respectful members of their future society, so I refused to sign it.

Here was a person that wanted to hijack the lives of boys and girls so that they remained stagnate in their personal development to improve themselves. Just like my husband's behaviour with his young work colleagues.

I worked in a man's world so would hear conversations from them about keeping women under control by giving them a smack. One said he wasn't going to pay his taxes so that a single mother could be assisted financially to get on her feet during the time she was responsible for a young child. Once her child was old enough and she could train into an earning position so that she would be paying taxes herself and a useful member of society.

These people that hold progress to ransom are not mentally mature enough to grasp the concept of a different perspective.

Society has progressed in recent years despite the conservative types that are afraid of change. We can advance to make changes for the better if we look at improvement for all of humanity, not just what can we get out of the change personally.

We now have acceptance of mental illness without holding us back. Offenders of violent acts need help just as much as their victims. Violent people have an illness that could be corrected by proper diagnosing and treatment.

I have learnt that my husband was suffering from a mental illness that was inherited and promoted as acceptable behaviour. The names given for this illness is varied.

Antisocial Personality Disorder. Psychopath, Sociopath. Frontal Brain Damage. Borderline Personality Disorder and Narcist Personality Disorder. They all have the same behavioural observations.

List of traits which can be found are: Violent Abuse, Aggression. Abnormal ways of thinking. Lack of Empathy. Calculated and strategic Planning. Detached cold and Callous Demeanour. Sadistic. Enjoyment of Pain and Suffering. Blame Game. Family Gossip. Biting Comments. Entertainment when they Hurt or Embarrass someone.

These were all traits I discovered in my Husband's behaviour toward myself and my children.

These are all indications of someone that needs Professional help. They should be avoided on a personal level so that you do not become their victim. These are traits that can be found in both Female and Male Personality Disorders. Don't be fooled into thinking it's a Male gender only.

During my marriage I felt very lonely, being surrounded by my Husband's Narcistic friends and his manipulation of my personal feelings.

We are not ourselves when we are triggered, we become who we think we need to be to survive and when we are constantly triggered our identity can start to slip away because our personality and values are hijacked by fight or flight reflexes.

I chose to stay so shame on me. I let my Husband walk all over me. I put up with his mind games. I believed that one day he would change and be capable of love and empathy. I allowed him to mislead me and thought that one day we might have a chance. I lived a fantasy of what could be when I gave him the opportunity to set me free, he let me down.

I used to think that the worst thing in life was to end up alone. It's not. The worst thing in life is to end up with people who make you feel alone. I was a tolerant, gentle, compassionate person. These traits are not weaknesses but are strengths.

I am now free of allowing others to control me. I live on my own. I have lived a successful, financially capable life. Some women aren't given financial freedom in their marriage. I was, if I provided financially for myself and children, and my Husband was free to live his life without having to provide for us.

My Children and Grandchildren will inherent some of the damage passed on by me and the ignorant society I grew up in. The positive side of the toxic behaviour in the family home is they have become resilient, capable and useful humans, assets to society as it is to-day.

Remember to take notice of your own instincts. Ignore the Do-gooders, Influencers, people that make you feel insignificant. Shine from the inside, reflect that beautiful soul you were born with, and you will attract intelligent people that see the soul not the body.

Don't argue with a mentally immature person. See them for what they are and walk away. There is no point to argue with them as they cannot grasp someone else's point of view.

I struggled through life but have become the person I want to be. Happy in my skin and free from toxic mind games.

The End

www.ingramcontent.com/pod-product-compliance
Lightning Source LLC
Chambersburg PA
CBHW041320110526
44591CB00021B/2849